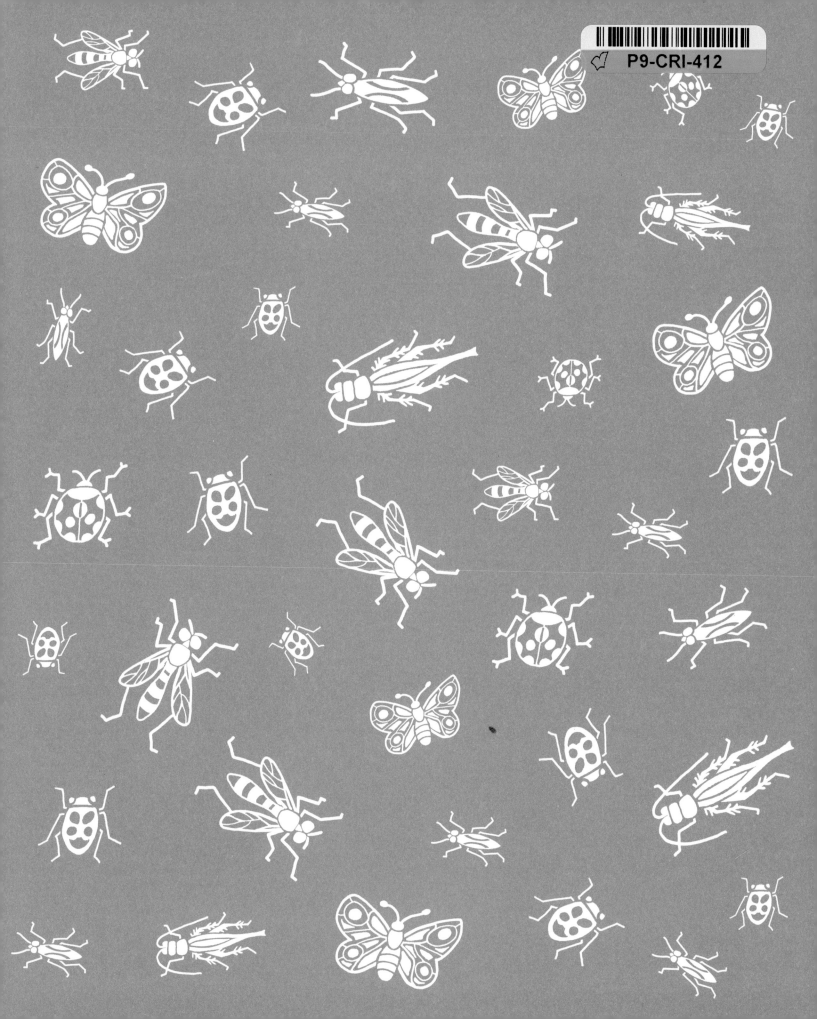

The Best Book of

Bugs

Claire Llewellyn

KINGFISHER

NEW YORK

Author: Claire Llewellyn
Consultant: Michael Chinery
Managing Editor: Camilla Hallinan
Series Editor: Sue Nicholson
Illustrators: Chris Forsey, Andrea
 Ricciardi di Gaudesi, David Wright
Art Editor: Christina Fraser
Art Director and cover design:
 Terry Woodley
Series Designer: Ben White
Production Controller: Kelly Johnson

Contents

KINGFISHER
Larousse Kingfisher Chambers Inc.
95 Madison Avenue
New York, New York 10016

First published in 1998

10 9 8 7 6 5 4 3 2 1

LIBRARY OF CONGRESS CATALOGING-IN-PUBLICATION DATA
Llewellyn, Claire.
    Bugs / Claire Llewellyn.—1st ed.
       p.   cm.
    Includes index
    Summary: Describes the habits and life cycles of various insects
and provides clues for identifying them in their natural habitats.
    1. Arthropoda—Juvenile literature. 2. Insects—Juvenile
literature. [1. Insects.]   I. Title.
QL437.2.L595   1998
595—dc21   97-39700   CIP AC

ISBN 0-7534-5118-2
Printed in Hong Kong

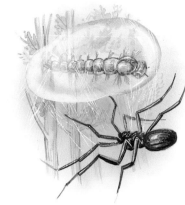

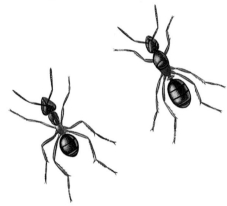

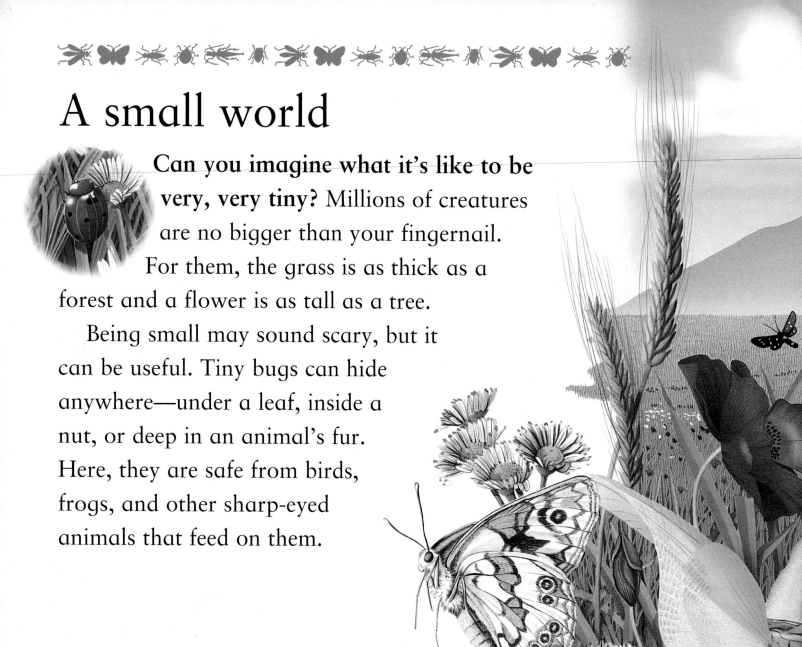

A small world

Can you imagine what it's like to be very, very tiny? Millions of creatures are no bigger than your fingernail.

For them, the grass is as thick as a forest and a flower is as tall as a tree.

Being small may sound scary, but it can be useful. Tiny bugs can hide anywhere—under a leaf, inside a nut, or deep in an animal's fur. Here, they are safe from birds, frogs, and other sharp-eyed animals that feed on them.

Hiding places

Bugs live all around us, yet most of the time we don't even know they are there. Look for them in places they like to hide— under a stone, inside a flowerpot, or in the crack of a wall.

A big collection

Flies

There are millions of different bugs and spiders, and they live all over the world. In fact, there are so many different kinds that scientists have sorted them into groups. Each group contains animals with the same kind of body plan.

This book looks at bugs (or insects) and spiders. All bugs and spiders have a hard casing on the outside of their bodies called the exoskeleton. This protects an animal's soft insides, just like a strong suit of armor.

Bugs

All the creatures on this page—the beetles, bee, butterfly, true bugs, flies, and ants—are bugs. There are more bugs in the world than any other kind of animal.

Butterfly

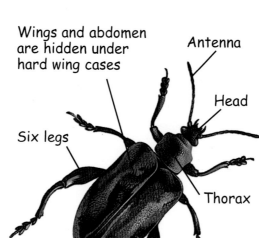
Wings and abdomen are hidden under hard wing cases

Antenna

Head

Six legs

Thorax

Beetle on the ground

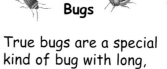
True Bugs

True bugs are a special kind of bug with long, beaky mouthparts

Many bugs look very different from one another, but they all have three pairs of legs and three parts to their bodies—the head, thorax, and abdomen. Many bugs also have wings, and most have long feelers called antennae.

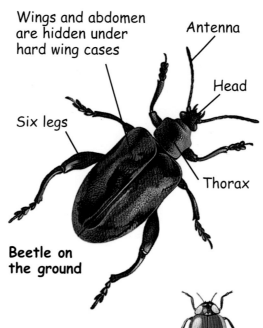
Beetle in flight

Wing case

Abdomen

Wing

Bee

A ladybug is a kind of beetle

Ants

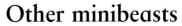

Spider

Millipede

Centipede

Other minibeasts

You'll spot other minibeasts in this book. They live in the same kind of places as spiders and bugs.

Centipedes and millipedes have long, wriggly bodies made up of segments. Centipedes have one pair of legs on each segment, millipedes have two.

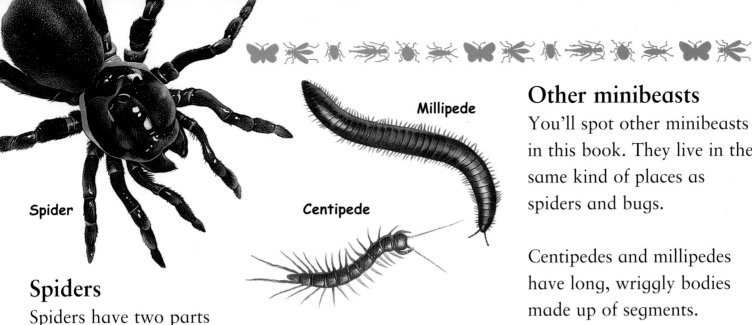

Abdomen

Eight legs

Head and thorax joined together

Spider

Palps—for feeling and tasting

Spiders

Spiders have two parts to their bodies—the head and thorax at the front, and the abdomen at the back. Spiders have four pairs of legs, one more pair than bugs.

Soil mites

Scorpions, mites, and ticks are closely related to spiders. Scorpions have two parts to their bodies, mites and ticks have one. Like spiders, they each have four pairs of legs.

Red velvet mites

Scorpion

Snail

Snails and slugs don't have legs. They crawl along on their soft bellies. Snails live inside a hard shell. Slugs get by without a shell.

Earthworms have long, soft bodies that are covered with tiny bristles. They don't have skeletons or shells to protect them. They live in soft, damp soil underground.

Earthworm

Spinning spiders

Spiders are amazing creatures.
They can make a silk that is stronger than steel, and weave it into beautiful, lacy webs. The webs are important because many spiders have poor eyesight, and their sticky traps help them catch their food. When an insect flies into the web, the spider feels it instantly through the hairs on its legs, and rushes over for the kill.

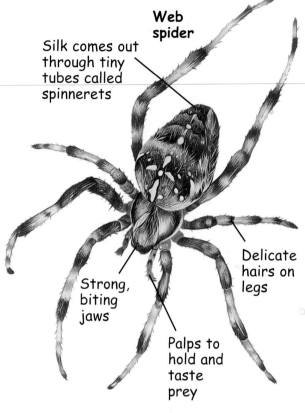

Web spider

Silk comes out through tiny tubes called spinnerets

Delicate hairs on legs

Strong, biting jaws

Palps to hold and taste prey

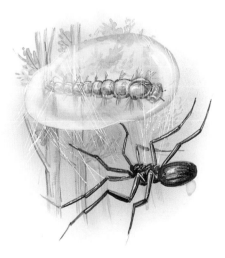

Sheet-web spider
A sheet-web spider spins a flat web with crisscrossing threads above it. Small bugs crash into the threads, and fall on the web below.

Net-casting spider
A net-casting spider hangs head-down and holds its silk web in its front legs. It throws the web over its prey like a net, to trap it.

Water spider
A water spider lives in a bell-shaped web under the surface of the water. It dashes out and seizes tiny creatures as they paddle by.

When a struggling bug is caught in its web, the spider injects it with poison and wraps it up tightly in silk. The poison kills the bug and turns it into a runny food, which the spider sucks up like a drink.

Spinning a web

Many spiders build a new web every day.

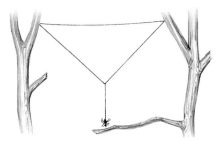

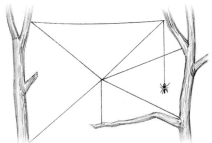

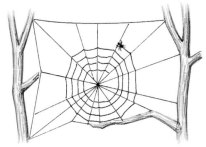

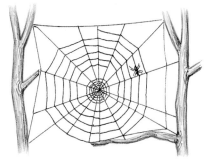

Garden spiders spin round orb webs. It usually takes them about an hour to do.

Hunting spiders

Hunting spiders chase, ambush, or leap on their prey. They don't use webs. They have sharp eyes to help them spot their prey, and strong legs to help them catch it. Their jaws are good for biting. Some spiders also use their jaws to dig burrows, where they hide and lie in wait.

Wandering spider

The wandering spider doesn't have a home. It is always on the move, hunting for a tasty cockroach or caterpillar.

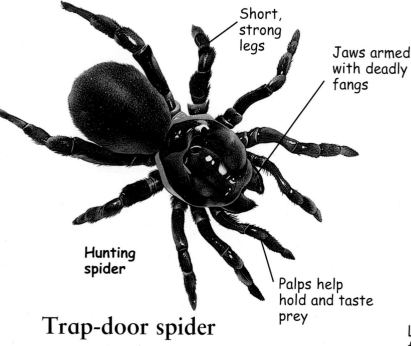

Short, strong legs

Jaws armed with deadly fangs

Hunting spider

Palps help hold and taste prey

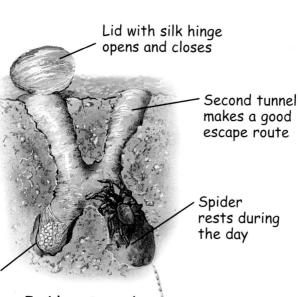

Lid with silk hinge opens and closes

Second tunnel makes a good escape route

Spider rests during the day

Leftovers from meal

Inside a trap-door spider's burrow

Trap-door spider

A trap-door spider builds an underground burrow by shoveling away the soil with its jaws. Then it lines the burrow with silk, covers it with a lid, and camouflages it with twigs and grass. The lid keeps out enemies and the rain.

Jumping spider
The sharp-eyed jumping spider stalks its prey like a cat, then suddenly pounces for the kill.

Bolas spider
The bolas spider catches bugs with a sticky line of silk, which it swings around like a lasso.

Spitting spider
The spitting spider traps bugs with a sticky gum fired through its fangs.

► At dusk, the trap-door spider lifts the lid of its burrow and waits. As soon as a creature passes by, the spider leaps out, stuns it with poison, and drags it back into its burrow to eat.

Buzzing bees

Honeybees are busy all summer long. They fly from flower to flower, feeding on the sweet nectar inside. There are many different kinds of bee. Most of them live on their own, in a burrow or a hollow stem. But honeybees live with thousands of others in a huge group called a colony. A colony works as a team. Together, the bees build a nest, find food, fight their enemies, and take care of their young.

A bees' nest

Honeybees build their nest in a cave or a hollow tree. Bees make a waxy material, which they shape into long slabs called honeycomb. Bees' nests are strong and may last 50 years or more.

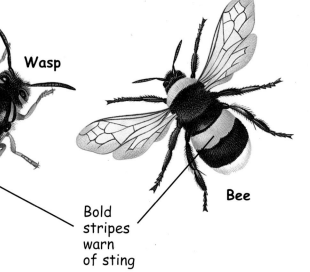

Wasp

Bee

Bold stripes warn of sting

Wasps' nest

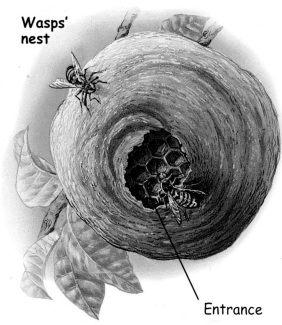

Entrance

A wasps' nest

Wasps live in colonies, too. Every year, they build a new nest out of thin sheets of paper. They make the paper themselves by chewing tiny pieces of wood and mixing it with their saliva. The nest has a small doorway, which is always guarded. The wasps keep their eggs and young safe inside.

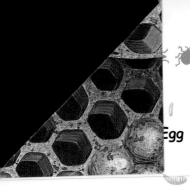

Egg

Young larva

Full-grown larva

Pupa

A honeybee's year

1 ▶ In a honeybees' nest, most of the bees are females, called workers. A few of the bees are males, called drones. One of the bees is a queen.

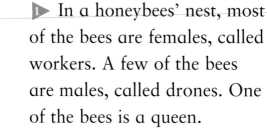

2 ◀ When she is young, the queen bee mates with the drones. Soon afterward, she begins to lay thousands of eggs. She lays each egg in its own little pocket, or cell, in the honeycomb.

Worker

3 ▶ After three days, the eggs hatch into wriggly grubs called larvae. The worker bees feed the larvae with nectar and pollen from flowers.

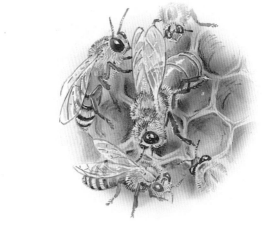

Drone

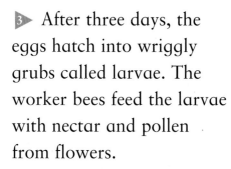

4 ◀ In a few days, the larvae are full grown and the workers seal their cells with wax. Inside, each larva changes into a pupa, which then becomes a bee.

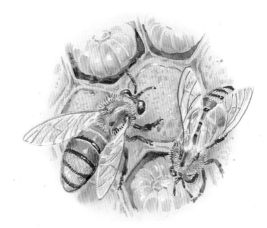

Queen

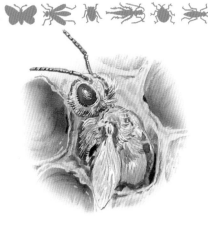

5 The new bees start work as soon as they hatch. They clean the nest, feed the queen, and take care of the next batch of eggs.

6 As they grow older, the young bees start to make wax and build new slabs of honeycomb to hold extra food supplies for the winter.

7 During the summer, the workers leave the nest to gather food. They suck sugary nectar from flowers with their long tongues.

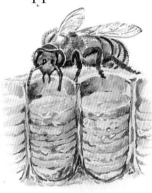

8 Pollen is a yellow dust made by flowers. As they eat, the bees comb pollen onto their back legs and carry it back to the nest.

9 Inside the nest, the nectar is turned into honey and is stored in the cells. The pollen is stored there too, in layers.

10 When a bee finds a new source of food, it returns to the nest and does a special dance to tell the other bees where they can find it too.

11 If a bees' nest gets too crowded, the old queen flies off with a swarm of workers to start a new nest. A larva in the old nest grows into a new queen.

12 Honeybees rest in the winter, feeding on their honey supply and keeping warm. In the spring, they fly off in search of more nectar.

Hardworking ants

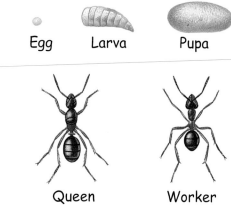

Egg   Larva   Pupa

Queen   Worker

Ants make their nests under large stones or plants. Each nest contains hundreds of ants. One of them, the queen, lays all the eggs. The others are workers. They do different jobs around the nest, such as feeding the larvae or gathering food. Ants eat all kinds of plants and animals. When they find food, they mark a trail back to the nest with a powerful scent, which the other ants quickly follow.

The queen ant

A queen ant has wings at first, but pulls them out after she flies off to mate with a male. She spends the rest of her life laying hundreds of eggs.

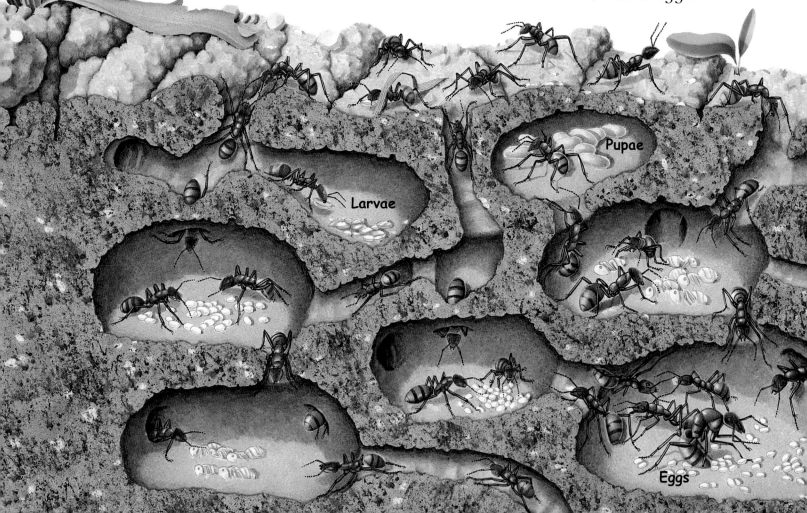

Pupae

Larvae

Eggs

An ants' nest

There are many different rooms inside an ants' nest. Some are nurseries for the eggs, larvae, and pupae. Others are used to store food or garbage.

Worker ants are always busy. Some take care of the queen and nurseries. Others guard the entrance to the nest, attack intruders, and search for food. Ants tap each other with their antennae to pass information.

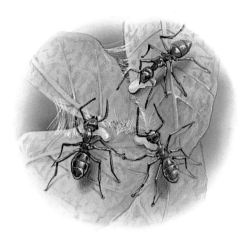

Weaver ants

Weaver ants work as a team to build their nest. Some of the ants hold leaves together. Others bind the edges of the leaves together with sticky, silky thread made by their larvae.

Honeypot ants

Honeypot ants use some of their workers as jars. When flowers are plentiful, they fill the workers with nectar. They "milk" them when food is harder to find.

Busy beetles

All kinds of beetles crawl over the woodland floor, busily looking for food. Some munch on plants. Others are hunters that kill and eat other creatures, or nibble on their rotting remains.

Beetles are small but very important. As they crawl and eat their way through the leaves, they mix dead plants and animals into the soil. This nourishes the soil, and helps new plants grow.

Many other bugs live in woodlands, too, because there is plenty of food.

Jaws

Stag beetle

A beetle's bite

Many beetles have powerful jaws for grabbing, biting, and chewing their prey. This stag beetle is a male. Its huge jaws look like horns or antlers. It uses them to fight other males.

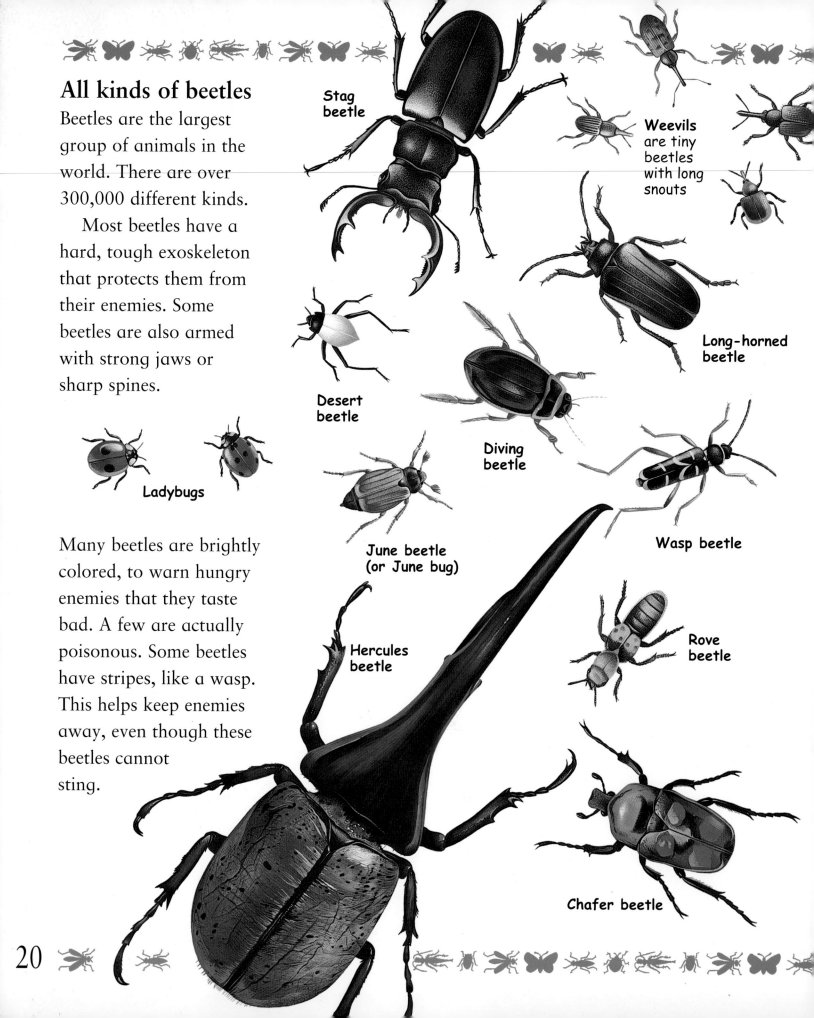

All kinds of beetles

Beetles are the largest group of animals in the world. There are over 300,000 different kinds.

Most beetles have a hard, tough exoskeleton that protects them from their enemies. Some beetles are also armed with strong jaws or sharp spines.

Many beetles are brightly colored, to warn hungry enemies that they taste bad. A few are actually poisonous. Some beetles have stripes, like a wasp. This helps keep enemies away, even though these beetles cannot sting.

Stag beetle

Weevils are tiny beetles with long snouts

Long-horned beetle

Desert beetle

Diving beetle

Ladybugs

June beetle (or June bug)

Wasp beetle

Hercules beetle

Rove beetle

Chafer beetle

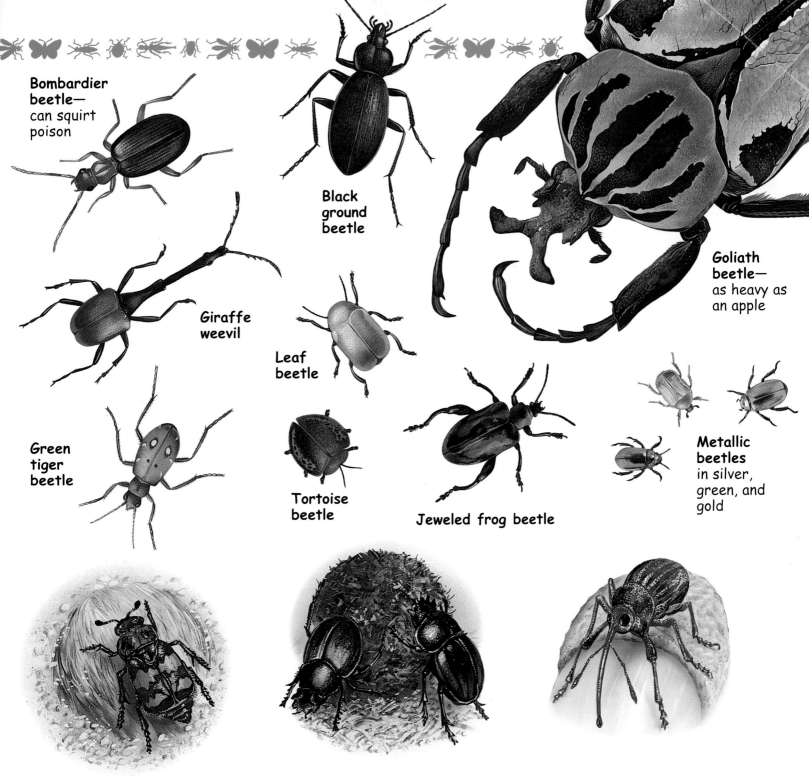

Bombardier beetle—
can squirt poison

Black ground beetle

Goliath beetle—
as heavy as an apple

Giraffe weevil

Leaf beetle

Green tiger beetle

Tortoise beetle

Jeweled frog beetle

Metallic beetles in silver, green, and gold

Burying beetles

Burying beetles bury dead animals and lay their eggs on top. Their tiny larvae then have plenty to eat.

Dung beetles

Dung beetles lay their eggs inside balls of animal dung, which they then bury under the ground.

Nut weevils

Nut weevils drill holes in nuts and lay their eggs inside. The larvae eat the nuts from the inside out.

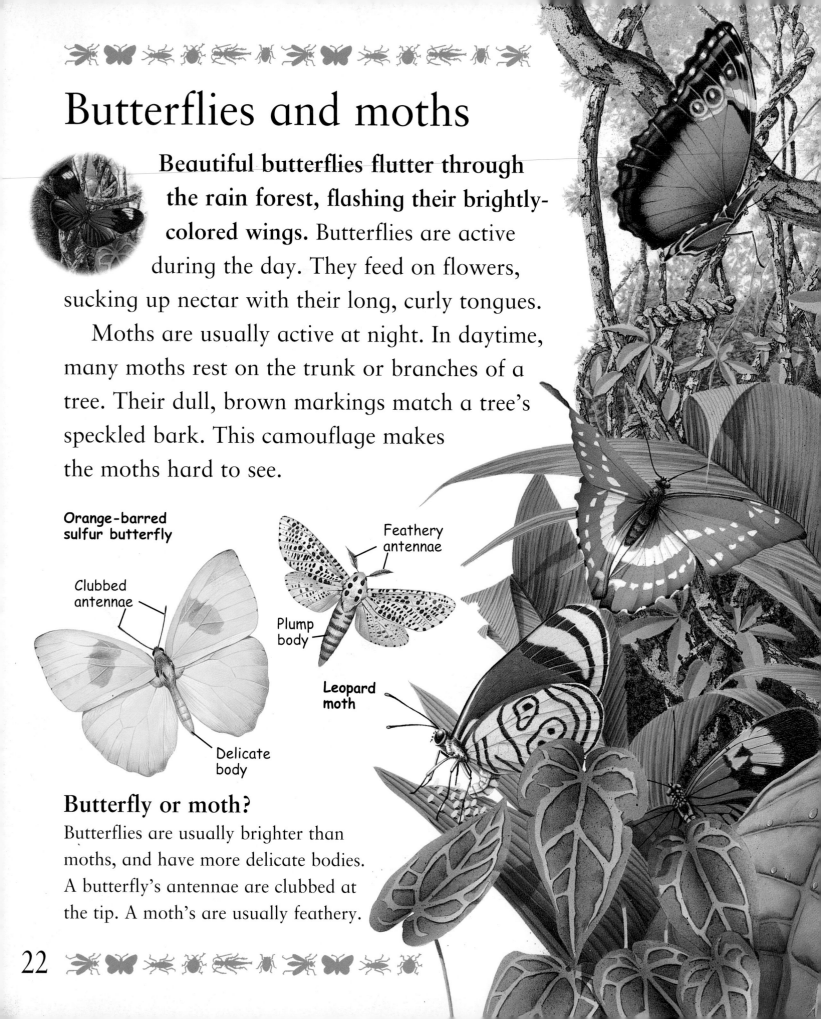

Butterflies and moths

Beautiful butterflies flutter through the rain forest, flashing their brightly-colored wings. Butterflies are active during the day. They feed on flowers, sucking up nectar with their long, curly tongues.

Moths are usually active at night. In daytime, many moths rest on the trunk or branches of a tree. Their dull, brown markings match a tree's speckled bark. This camouflage makes the moths hard to see.

Orange-barred sulfur butterfly

Clubbed antennae

Delicate body

Feathery antennae

Plump body

Leopard moth

Butterfly or moth?

Butterflies are usually brighter than moths, and have more delicate bodies. A butterfly's antennae are clubbed at the tip. A moth's are usually feathery.

Egg to butterfly

There are about 150,000 kinds of butterflies and moths, and they and their caterpillars come in all sorts of colors and sizes.

The Atlas moth is as big as a dinner plate. The Western pygmy blue butterfly is not much wider than your thumb.

Butterflies, like many bugs, change completely as they grow. This change is called metamorphosis.

Red admiral butterfly lays egg on leaf

Caterpillar hatches from egg

Caterpillar changes into pupa

Butterfly dries wings in the air

Madagascan sunset moth

Apollo butterfly

Western pygmy blue butterfly

Luna moth

Cabbage white butterfly and caterpillar

Cairn's birdwing butterfly and caterpillar

Gypsy moth

88 butterfly

Red admiral butterfly

Orange-tip butterfly

Atlas moth—the largest moth in the world

Swallowtail butterfly and caterpillar

Smooth emerald moth

Comma butterfly and caterpillar

Common blue butterfly and caterpillar

Owl moth

Hornet moth

Bright wings

The wings of butterflies and moths are covered with tiny scales that shimmer in the light. Some of them are brightly colored. Others have bold patterns or scary eyespots. When a butterfly or moth flashes its wings at its enemies, it confuses them, and gives itself time to escape.

Darting dragonflies

Life in a pond is not as peaceful as it seems. Huge dragonflies dart noisily through the air, snatching at flies. Dainty damselflies flash like jewels in the sun as they snap at gnats and midges. Other hunters live in the water itself, and pounce on anything that moves.

Egg to dragonfly

A dragonfly begins its life as an egg in the water. The egg hatches into a fierce creature called a nymph, which lives and grows in the pond. After a year or two, the nymph climbs out of the water onto a plant. There its skin splits open, and a new dragonfly crawls out. Not every small creature leaves the pond. Some, like water scorpions and spiders, spend their entire lives under the water.

Catching a meal

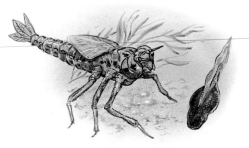

1 A dragonfly nymph lurks deep in the pond, hidden by its muddy colors. Suddenly a tadpole swims past.

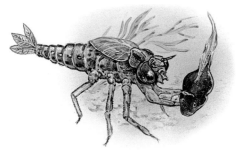

2 Quickly, the nymph shoots out a pair of sharp, hooked jaws and grabs its prey.

▶ A dragonfly is a powerful flier. It has two pairs of wings, and each pair works on its own. This helps the dragonfly twist, turn, change its speed, or hover over the water.

3 The nymph's deadly jaws slide back to its mouth, and the hunter feeds on its catch.

Strong, chewing mouthparts

Huge eyes to spot its prey

Hooked jaw hidden under head

Two pairs of gauzy wings

Dragonfly nymph

Adult dragonfly

Damselfly
nymph

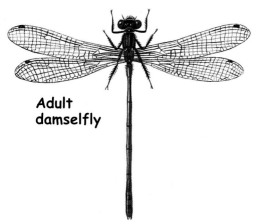

Adult
damselfly

▲ Like dragonflies, damselflies and caddis flies lay their eggs in ponds. A damselfly egg hatches into a nymph. A caddis fly egg hatches into a larva.

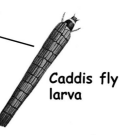

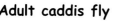

Larva hides in a silk tube, which it camouflages with plants and stones

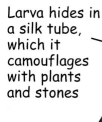

Caddis fly larva

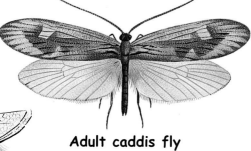

Adult caddis fly

Living on water

All animals need oxygen. Some pond creatures get oxygen from the water. Others get it from the air.

A damselfly nymph has three gills on its tail, which soak up oxygen in water.

A water scorpion floats to the surface of the water and takes in air through a tube.

A diving beetle collects air bubbles and stores them under its wings.

Out at night

Summer nights are alive with all kinds of bugs. Crickets chirp, mosquitoes hum, and tiny fireflies flash in the dark. This is their way of sending signals to each other.

Night is a good time for bugs because the air is cool, and many of their enemies are asleep. Through the hours of darkness, these tiny creatures feed, hunt, and look for a mate. At dawn they hide, and the bees, butterflies, and other sun-loving creatures return with the warmth and light.

Glossary

abdomen The back part of a bug's body. Inside the abdomen is the heart, and the various parts that break down food and help a creature produce its young.

antenna (*plural* antennae) One of a pair of feelers that pick up scents and tastes in the air, and help an animal feel its way around.

bug (or insect) An animal with three parts to its body and three pairs of jointed legs.

camouflage The colors and markings on an animal that help it blend in with its surroundings and make it difficult to see.

colony A large group of animals that live together. Honeybees live in a colony. So do ants.

drone A male honeybee, whose only job is to mate with the queen.

exoskeleton The hard casing on the outside of the body of most bugs.

fang The clawlike part of a spider's jaws that it uses to stick into an animal and inject poison.

gill The part of an animal's body that allows it to breathe under water. The gills soak up oxygen that has dissolved in water. The nymphs of water bugs, such as damselflies, have gills.

grub Another name for the legless larva of an insect.

larva (*plural* larvae) The young stage of an insect after it hatches out of an egg, which looks very different from the adult. A larva has to pass through a pupa stage before it becomes an adult bug.

metamorphosis The change from a young bug into an adult bug—for example, from a caterpillar to a butterfly.

nectar The sugary juice inside flowers that attracts bugs and other small animals. Bees use nectar to make honey.

nymph The young stage of a bug, such as a grasshopper or a dragonfly, that changes gradually into an adult without passing through a pupa stage.

oxygen A gas that all animals need to breathe in order to survive. Oxygen is one of the gases found in the air, and in water.

palp One of a pair of feelers near the jaws of a spider or a bug that feel and taste its food.

pollen The yellow dustlike powder made by flowers. When bugs carry it to other flowers of the same kind, they can make seeds.

pupa (*plural* pupae) The stage in a bug's life when it changes from a larva to an adult. In butterflies and moths, the pupa is called the chrysalis.

thorax The middle part of a bug's body, in between the head and the abdomen. A bug's wings and legs are attached to the thorax.

true bug A group of bugs with a long, sharp feeding tube, that they use to pierce animals or plants and suck out their juices.